Writings of Augustine

Upper Room Spiritual Classics®

Selected, edited, and introduced by
KEITH BEASLEY-TOPLIFFE

UPPER
ROOM BOOKS®
NASHVILLE

WRITINGS OF AUGUSTINE
Copyright © 1997 by Upper Room Books
Previously published as *Hungering for God: Selected Writings of Augustine*
All rights reserved.

Upper Room Books' website: books.upperroom.org

Cover design: Tim Green | Faceout Studio
Interior design and typesetting: PerfecType, Nashville, TN

ISBN 978-0-8358-1643-4 (print) | ISBN 978-0-8358-1669-4 (mobi) | ISBN 978-0-8358-1670-0 (epub)

Library of Congress Cataloging-in-Publication Data

Augustine, Saint, Bishop of Hippo.
   [Selections. English. 1997]
   Hungering for God: selected writings of Augustine,
     p. cm.—(Upper Room spiritual classics. Series 1)
   Includes bibliographical references.
   ISBN 0-8358-0830-0 (pbk.)
   1. Augustine, Saint, Bishop of Hippo. 2. Christian saints—Algeria—Hippo (Extinct city)—Biography. 3. Spiritual life—Christianity—Early works to 1800. I. Title. II. Series.
BR65.A52E6 1997
270.2—dc21   97-9244
                                          CIP

Contents

Introduction

It is hard to exaggerate the importance in Western church history of Aurelius Augustinus, better known as Augustine. The bishop of Hippo (now Annaba on Algeria's Mediterranean coast) played a key role during the waning years of the Roman Empire. Augustine's training as a rhetorician (professional speaker), his extensive reading in philosophy, and his fascination with Scripture combined to make him the ideal defender of the faith in his time. His extensive writings became the foundation for all later developments in theology in the Middle Ages and during the Reformation. Although the Reformation is often described as an effort to get behind later developments to the early church and the Bible itself, one could also see it as an attempt to get past commentaries on Augustine to "the authentic teaching of Augustine himself."*

Augustine is equally important as a spiritual writer. He looked into the depths of his own soul to gain understanding of the workings of sin and grace in his own life. He shared

---

*Jaroslav Pelikan, *Reformation of Church and Dogma (1300–1700),* vol. 4 of *The Christian Tradition: A History of the Development of Doctrine* (Chicago: The University of Chicago Press, 1983), 22.

these findings, not only in his autobiographical *Confessions,* but also in his preaching and other writings. His descriptions of the extent of sin before his conversion and the persistence of sin afterward have offered encouragement to many who worried that their own sinful past or present imperfection might turn God away from them. His portrait of his attempts to resist God's call can hold a mirror to our own struggles and excuses.

Augustine's World

Augustine lived during the last years of the western Roman Empire. Barbarian armies were steadily pressing in from the north. In 408, when Augustine was fifty-four, the city of Rome was sacked and burned by an army of Goths. Although the end did not come until 467, the signs were clear. In many parts of the empire, the official channels of government were much less important than the patronage of rich individuals who could control their immediate neighborhoods.

Christianity had been legalized in 313 and soon became the official religion of the empire. In 341, pagan sacrifices were outlawed. But the victory was far from complete. Many held that Christianity—or at least the abandonment of the old gods—was the reason for the decline of the empire. During Augustine's childhood, the emperor Julian (d. 363) had attempted to restore paganism. He also promoted dissension among Christians by restoring bishops who had been exiled for heresy.

Though Julian's efforts died with him, the church remained in turmoil. Theology was still in flux. Many groups denounced one another as heretics. The Arians (named for Arius, a preacher from Alexandria who died ca. 336) held that Christ was a godlike creature but not God. Several emperors and many of the barbarian tribes supported the Arians, and there were Arian churches as well as Catholic ones in Rome and Milan in Augustine's day. The Donatists (named for Donatus, a bishop in Carthage in the early fourth century) held that the validity of sacraments was dependent upon the sanctity of the priest or bishop performing them. In particular, they rejected all clergy who had weakened in the face of persecution. This movement was strongest in North Africa around Carthage, the area where Augustine spent most of his life. The Pelagian movement began in the 380s as a lay movement and got its name from Pelagius, a British priest and theologian who went to Italy and then to Jerusalem. The Pelagians held that our efforts to save ourselves (through right living) are more important than God's grace—an issue that has continued to divide the church. Augustine wrote extensively against the Pelagians.

Perhaps the most important heresy in Augustine's own life, though, was Manicheism. Mani was a third-century Persian who declared himself to be the incarnation of the Holy Spirit and offered a series of revelations on the nature of God, humanity, and the universe. The sect spread rapidly eastward to India and China and westward throughout the Roman Empire. Manichees held a dualistic view of a power of evil over against the good God whom Jesus called Father. Satan had imprisoned divine "sparks" within sinful flesh, they said. The only "cure" was to hate the flesh and resist every desire. Augustine spent a decade as an "auditor" of the Manichees, never quite making the commitment to become one of the "elect."

Augustine's Life

Augustine was born in Thagaste (today Souk Ahras in Algeria near the Tunisian border) in 354. His father, Patricius, was poor but had family connections that enabled him to educate his son—the road to advancement in the government bureaucracy. His mother, Monica, was a Christian whose two great hopes seem to have been for her son to convert and for him to marry a rich heiress whose wealth would allow him leisure.

Augustine studied in Madauros, then finished in Carthage (today's Tunis). While in Carthage he discovered philosophy through the writings of Cicero and became involved with the Manichees. Their teachings about the divine spark's captivity in flesh supported his own feeling that his sexual urges were uncontrollable. At eighteen he took a mistress or concubine with whom he lived for the next twelve years. They had one son, Adeodatus, who died when he was sixteen. During the time in Carthage, Augustine's father died and Monica moved in with Augustine.

Augustine returned to Thagaste to teach, but the death of his best friend caused him to leave home forever and return to Carthage. There he met one of the leaders of the Manichees and found him disappointingly unlearned. In 383, he left for Rome and soon was appointed to teach rhetoric in Milan, where the emperor and his court lived. In Milan he began to listen to the preaching of the bishop, Ambrose, and enrolled as a catechumen in preparation for baptism. Meanwhile, Monica had finally found the right girl for her thirty-year-old son. Unfortunately she was only eight, two years short of legal marrying age. A condition of the engagement was that Augustine dismiss his mistress, a painful break after a dozen years. He consoled himself with more temporary arrangements. He also gathered a group of friends who lived and studied together. A visitor to this household talked about Antony who had gone into the Egyptian desert to flee from worldly temptations and take on Satan directly. This story so affected Augustine that his own excuses for sin broke down and he was converted. He was baptized by Ambrose on Easter Eve, 387.

Augustine and his friends returned to Africa in hope of setting up a monastic community. Monica died on the way. Augustine also began to write. Many of his earliest works were against the Manichees. His plans for a quiet scholarly life were interrupted when, during a visit to Hippo, he was seized by a crowd that demanded he be made a priest. (This was a common occurrence in those days. Ambrose had gone from catechumen through baptism and ordination to bishop in a few days at the urging of a similar mob.) Soon the bishop of Hippo, Valerius, made Augustine his assistant and designated successor. So, in 395, Augustine became bishop of Hippo. As bishop he continued to write, teach, and preach. His first major work after becoming bishop was the *Confessions,* published in 397. Augustine served as judge or mediator, not only for Christians, but also for pagans who considered him fair and impartial. He engaged in public debates with Manichees, Donatists, and Pelagians. He also carried on an extensive correspondence. He wrote regularly to Jerome, who was in Jerusalem preparing what was to become the standard Latin translation of the Bible. The sack of Rome in 408 revived muttering that Christianity was bringing the destruction of the empire. In response Augustine wrote his longest work, *The City of God.* In it, he compared the two cities that have existed since creation: the city of this world and the city of God, arguing that the fortunes of the first are not ultimately important to the citizens of the second. Barbarians continued to make raids deep into the empire. Vandals were attacking Hippo itself when Augustine died there on August 28, 430.

Further Reading

Augustine's writings come to more than a thousand "books." (A book is roughly equivalent to a chapter in a modern book. *Confessions,* for example, has thirteen books. *The City of God* has twenty-two.) Many of Augustine's writings, letters, and sermons are available in English translation, though most are in expensive scholarly collections. *Confessions* and *The City of God* are available in paperback in several editions. A biography by Peter Brown, *Augustine of Hippo,* is very thorough.

The story of Antony that was important in Augustine's conversion was written by Athanasius (d. 373) and is available in modern translation from Paulist Press.

Note on the Text

These selections from Augustine are based on a series of translations produced in Scotland during the 1870s and reprinted in *The Nicene and Post-Nicene Fathers, Series I,* as volumes one through eight. The language has been modernized in consultation with later translations and with the original Latin. The selections have also been edited for length and for inclusive language. Augustine quotes Scripture constantly and often quite freely usually, but not always, using Jerome's translation. As far as possible, the quotations and allusions have been conformed to the language of the New Revised Standard Version and are indicated by *italics* in the text.

Created to Love God

From *Confessions,* Book I, 1, 2, 4–6

Augustine wrote the Confessions *in 397, two years after becoming bishop of Hippo. The first nine (of thirteen) books tell the story of his life from birth until shortly after his conversion at age thirty-two. The work is addressed to God as both confession of sin and confession of faith, though Augustine is also writing for the benefit of human readers. He begins with a song of praise.*

Great are you, O *Lord, and greatly to be praised;* great is your power, and your *understanding is beyond measure.* And people, being a part of your creation, desire to praise you—people who bear about with them their mortality, the witness of their sin, even the witness that you *oppose the proud.* Nevertheless, people, this part of your creation, desire to praise you. You move us to delight in praising you; for you have formed us for yourself, and our hearts are restless till they find rest in you. Lord, teach me to know and understand which of these should be first, to call on you or to praise you; and likewise to know you or to call upon you. But who is there that calls upon you without knowing you? For one who does not know you may call upon you as other than you are. Or perhaps we call on you that we may know you. *But how are they to call on one in whom they have not believed? . . . And how are they to hear without someone to proclaim him?* And *those who seek him shall praise the Lord.* For those who seek shall find God, and those who find God shall praise God. Let me seek you, Lord, in calling on you, and call on you in believing in you; for you have been preached to us. O Lord, my faith calls on you—that faith which you have imparted to me, which you have breathed into me through the incarnation of your Son, through the ministry of your preacher.

And how shall I call upon my God—my God and my Lord? For when I call on God, I ask God to come into me. What place is there in me into which my God can come, the God who made heaven and earth? Is there anything in me, O Lord my God, that can contain you? Do indeed heaven and earth, which you have made and in which you have made me, contain you? Or, as nothing could exist without you, does whatever exists contain you? Why, then, do I ask you to come into me, since I indeed exist and could not exist if you were not in me? Because I am not yet in hell, though you are even there; for *if I make my bed in hell you are there.* I could not therefore exist, could not exist at all, O my God, unless you were in me. Or should I not rather say that I could not exist unless I were in you *from whom and through whom and to whom are all things?* Even so, Lord, even so. Where do I call you to, since you are in me, or from where can you come into me? For where outside heaven and earth can I go that from that place my God may come into me who has said, *"I fill heaven and earth"*!

What, then, are you, O my God—what, I ask, but the Lord God? For who is Lord but the Lord? Who is God save our God? Most high, most excellent, most potent, most omnipotent; most merciful and most just; most hidden and most near; most beautiful and most strong; unchangeable, yet changing all things; never new, never old; making all things new, yet bringing old age upon the proud; always working, yet ever at rest; gathering, yet needing nothing; sustaining, pervading, and protecting; creating, nourishing, and developing; seeking, and yet possessing all things. You love without lusting; are jealous, yet free from care; repent, and have no sorrow; are angry, yet serene; change your ways, leaving your plans unchanged; recover what you find without ever losing; are never in want, while you rejoice in gain; never greedy, though requiring interest. You pay debts while owing nothing; and when you forgive debts, you lose nothing. Yet, O my God, my life, my holy joy, what is this that I have said? And what does anyone say who speaks of you? Yet woe to them that keep silence, seeing that even those who say the most are like those who do not speak at all.

Oh, how shall I find rest in you? Who will send you into my heart to inebriate it, so that I may forget my woes and embrace you as my only good? What are you to me? Have compassion on me, that I may speak. What am I to you that you demand my love? Unless I give it you are angry, and threaten me with great sorrows. Is it, then, a light sorrow not to love you? Alas, alas! Tell me of your compassion, O Lord my God, what you are to me. *Say to my soul, "I am your salvation."* So speak that I may hear. Behold, Lord, the ears of my heart are before you; open them. When I hear, may I run and lay hold on you. *Do not hide your face from me.* Let me die, if only I may see your face.

My soul's house is cramped. Expand it, so that you may enter in. It is in ruins. Restore it. It must offend your eyes. I confess and know it, but who will cleanse it? To whom shall I cry but to you? *Clear me from hidden faults,* O Lord, *and keep back your servant also from* those of others. I believe, and therefore I speak. Lord, you know. Did I not *confess my transgressions* to you, O my God? *You forgave the guilt of my* heart. I do not contend in judgment with you, who are the Truth. I would not deceive myself, lest my iniquity lie against itself. I do not, therefore, contend in judgment with you, *for if you, O Lord, should mark iniquities, Lord, who could stand?*

A Wild Teenager

From *Confessions*, Book II, 2–4, 7–8

When Augustine was fifteen, his father ran out of funds to support his education. Augustine had to come home. For a year he had little to do but amuse himself with a gang of friends and with sexual discovery. He reflects on how much freedom God allowed him without ever giving up on him.

What did I delight in but to love and to be beloved? But I did not hold the bright path of friendship in moderation, mind to mind. Instead, out of the dark desire of the flesh and the effervescence of youth came exhalations that obscured and overcast my heart. I was unable to discern pure affection from unholy desire. Both boiled confusedly within me, dragged away my unstable youth into the rough places of unchaste desires, and plunged me into a gulf of infamy. Your anger had overshadowed me and I did not know it. I became deaf by the rattling of the chains of my mortality, the punishment for my soul's pride. I wandered farther from you, and you allowed me. I was tossed to and fro, wasted and poured out, boiled over in my fornications, and you held your peace. O you, my tardy joy!

You held your peace and I wandered still farther from you, into more and more barren seed plots of sorrows, with proud dejection and restless lethargy.

If only someone would have regulated my disorder and turned to my profit the fleeting beauties of the things around me and set a boundary to their sweetness. Then the tides of my youth might have spent themselves upon the shore of married life, if they could not be tranquilized and satisfied within the object of raising a family, as your law appoints, O Lord. Thus you form the offspring of our mortality and, with a tender hand, blunt the thorns that were excluded from your paradise! For your omnipotence is not far from us even when we are far from you, or truly I would have listened more vigilantly to the voice from the clouds: *"Yet those who marry will experience distress in this life, and I would spare you that,"* and, *"It is well for a man not to touch a woman,"* and, *"The unmarried man is anxious about the affairs of the Lord, how to please the Lord; but the married man is anxious about the affairs of the world, how to please his wife."* I should, therefore, have listened more attentively to these words, and, being *made a eunuch for the sake of the kingdom of heaven,* I would have expected your embraces with greater happiness.

But I, poor fool, seethed like the sea. Forsaking you, I followed the violent course of my own stream and exceeded all your limitations. Nor did I escape your scourges. For what mortal can do so? But you were always by me, mercifully angry, and dashing all my illicit pleasures with the bitterest irritations so that I might seek pleasures free from irritation. But where I could meet such pleasures apart from you, O Lord, I could not find, except in you. You teach by sorrow and wound us to heal us and kill us that we may not die from you. Where was I, and how far was I exiled from the delights of your house, in that sixteenth year of mine, when the madness of lust—which human shamelessness grants full freedom, although forbidden by your laws—held complete sway over me? I gave myself to it completely. Those about me took no care to save me from ruin by marriage. Their sole concern was that I should learn to make powerful speeches and become a persuasive orator.

Woe is me! Dare I affirm that you held your peace, O my God, while I strayed farther from you? Then whose words were they but yours that you poured into my ears by my mother, your faithful servant? None of them sank into my heart to make me act. For I remember that she privately warned me with great concern, "Do not commit fornication; but above all things never commit adultery." This appeared to me mere womanly advice, which I should blush to obey. But it was your advice, though I did not know it. I thought that you held your peace, and that it was she who spoke. Through her you did not hold your peace toward me, and in her person you were despised by me, her son, *the child of your serving girl.* But I did not know this and rushed on headlong with such blindness that among my equals I was ashamed to be less shameless, when I heard them congratulating themselves for their disgraceful acts, and glorying all the more the lower they sank. I took pleasure in doing it, not for the pleasure's sake only, but for the praise. What is worthy of condemnation but vice? But I made myself out worse than I was, in order that I might not be blamed. When in anything I had not sinned like those abandoned ones, I would affirm that I had done what I had not, that I might not appear contemptible for being more innocent or of less esteem for being more chaste.

See what companions I had as I walked the streets of Babylon, in whose filth I rolled as if in cinnamon and precious ointments. That I might cling the more tenaciously to its very center, my invisible enemy trod me down and seduced me. I was easily seduced. My mother had already *fled from the midst of Babylon* and knew my behavior to be destructive in the present and dangerous in the future. Nevertheless, in counseling me to chastity she did not attempt to restrain my behavior within the limits of married affection—if it could not be cut away to the quick. She was afraid that a wife would prove a hindrance and a clog to my hopes. I do not mean those hopes of the future world, which my mother had in you; but the hope of learning, which both my parents were too anxious that I should acquire. My father had little or no thought of you, and but vain thoughts for me. My mother thought that ordinary learning would not only be no drawback, but a help toward my attaining you. That is my guess, as well as I can recall the dispositions of my parents. The reins, meantime, were slack-ened toward me, so that I might play in whatever I fancied. And in all there was a mist, shutting out from my sight the brightness of your truth, O my God.

Stolen Pears

From *Confessions*, Book II, 9–10, 12–13

In looking back on his sixteenth year, one event stands out for Augustine: the theft of some pears from a neighbor's tree. Remembering it leads him into a general discussion of sin and how easily we are deceived into finding sin attractive.

Theft is punished by your law, O Lord, and by the law written in our hearts, which iniquity itself cannot blot out. For what thief will tolerate being robbed by another thief? Even a rich thief will not put up with one who is driven to it by poverty. I had a desire to commit robbery and did so, compelled neither by hunger nor poverty but through a distaste for well-doing and a love of iniquity. For I stole something of which I had already enough, and much better. Nor did I desire to enjoy what I stole, but the theft and sin itself. There was a pear tree close to our vineyard, heavily laden with fruit, which was tempting for neither its color nor its flavor. Some of us reckless young fellows went to shake and rob it late one night (having, according to our disgraceful habit, prolonged our games in the streets until then). We carried away great loads, not to eat ourselves, but to throw at pigs, having only eaten some of them. That it was not permitted pleased us all the more. Behold my heart, O my God. Behold my heart, which you had pity on when it was in the bottomless pit. Let my heart tell you what it was seeking there, that I should be so freely reckless, having no inducement to evil but the evil itself. It was foul, and I loved it. I loved to perish. I loved my own error—not that for which I erred, but the error itself. Base soul, falling from your firmament to utter destruction—not seeking anything through the shame but the shame itself.

There is an attraction in all beautiful objects, and in gold and silver and all things. Worldly honor also has its glory, as do the power of command and conquering. From these proceeds also the desire for revenge. And yet to acquire all these, we must not depart from you, O Lord, nor deviate from your law. The life that we live here also has its own attractions, through a certain beauty of its own and harmony with all things here below. Human friendships also are endeared by a sweet bond, in the oneness of many souls. On account of all these, and such as these, sin is committed. Through an inordinate preference for these goods of a lower kind, the better and higher are neglected—even you, our Lord God, and your truth and your law. Yes, these lower things have their delights, but not like my God, who has created all things. *Let the righteous rejoice in the Lord . . . let the upright in heart glory.*

What was it, then, that I, miserable one, so doted on in you, you theft of mine, you deed of darkness, in that sixteenth year of my age? You were not beautiful, since you were theft. But are you anything, that I may argue the case with you? Those pears that we stole were fair to the sight, because they were your creation, you fairest of all, Creator of all, you good God—God, the highest good and my true good. Those pears truly were pleasant to the sight; but it was not for them that my miserable soul lusted. I had an abundance of better ones. Those I plucked simply that I might steal. For having plucked them, I threw them away, my sole gratification in them being my own sin, which I was pleased to enjoy. If any of those pears entered my mouth, the sweetener of it was my sin in eating it. And now, O Lord my God, I ask what it was in that theft of mine that caused me such delight. It has no beauty in it—not such, I mean, as exists in justice and wisdom; nor such as is in the mind, memory, senses, and animal life of a person; nor yet such as is the glory and beauty of the stars in their courses; or the earth, or the sea, teeming with new life, to replace, as it is born, that which decays; not even the false and shadowy beauty which deceptive vices seem to have.

Pride, for instance, imitates high estate, but you alone are God, high above all. And what does ambition seek but honors and renown, while you alone are to be honored above all and renowned forevermore? The cruelty of the powerful wishes to be feared; but who is to be feared but God only? For what can be snatched away or withdrawn from your power—when, or where, or how, or by whom? The enticements of the prostitute try to seem like love; and yet nothing is more enticing than your love, nor is anything loved more healthfully than your truth, bright and beautiful above all. Curiosity pretends a desire for knowledge, whereas it is you who supremely know all things. Yes, ignorance and foolishness are concealed under the names of innocence and harmlessness, because nothing can be found more innocent than you and what is more harmless, since harm comes to evil persons through their own works? Sloth seems to long for rest but what sure rest is there besides the Lord? Luxury wants to be called plenty and abundance, but you are the fullness and unfailing plenty of unfading joys. Wastefulness presents a shadow of generosity, but you are the most lavish giver of all good. Covetousness desires to possess much. You are the possessor of all things. Envy contends for excellence. What is so excellent as you? Anger seeks revenge. Who avenges more justly than you? Fear jumps at unexpected and sudden happenings that threaten beloved things and is careful for their security. But what can happen that is unexpected or sudden to you? Who can deprive you of what you love? Where is there unshaken security except with you? Grief languishes for things lost in which desire had delighted itself. But nothing can be lost by you.

Monica Finds Comfort in a Dream

From *Confessions*, Book III, 19–21

Augustine went to Carthage to finish his education. There he was introduced to philosophy through the works of Cicero. He began to be attracted to the Manichees. At the age of eighteen he took a concubine by whom he had a son, Adeodatus. When his father died, his mother, Monica, joined him in Carthage. She was deeply worried about the directions Augustine's life was taking.

You *stretched out your hand from on high,* and *delivered my soul from the depths* of darkness when my mother, your faithful one, wept to you on my behalf more than mothers weep the bodily death of their children. For by the faith and spirit that she had from you, she saw that I was dead, and you heard her, O Lord. You heard her and did not reject her tears when, pouring down, they watered the earth under her eyes in every place where she prayed. Yes, you heard her. From where did that dream come with which you consoled her, so that she permitted me to live with her and to have my meals at the same table in the house, which she had begun to avoid, hating and detesting the blasphemies of my error? She saw herself standing on a wooden ruler, and a bright youth advancing toward her, joyous and smiling on her, while she was grieving and bowed down with sorrow. He asked her the cause of her sorrow and daily weeping, and she answered that she was lamenting my perdition. He told her to relax and see "that where she was, there was I also." And when she looked she saw me standing near her on the same ruler. Where did this come from, unless your ears were inclined toward her heart? O Good Omnipotent, you care for each one of us as if you cared for that one only, and for all as if they were but one!

When she had narrated this vision to me, I tried to put this construction on it: That she should not despair of being someday what I was. Without hesitation she immediately replied, "No; because I was not told 'Where he is, there shall you be,' but 'Where you are, there shall he be.'" I confess to you, O Lord, that, to the best of my remembrance, your answer through my watchful mother moved me more than the dream itself. She was not upset by my false interpretation and saw in a moment what was to be seen, and which I myself had not perceived before she spoke. Yet by that dream that pious woman's happiness, to be realized so long after, was, for the alleviation of her present anxiety, predicted so long before. Yet nearly nine years passed in which I wallowed *in deep mire* and the darkness of falsehood, striving often to rise, but being all the more heavily dashed down. Yet that chaste, pious, and sober widow, now more buoyed up with hope, though no less zealous in her weeping and mourning, continued at every hour of prayer to bewail my case to you. Her *prayers came before you,* yet you still allowed me to be involved and re-involved in that darkness.

Meanwhile, you granted her another answer by a priest of yours, a certain bishop, reared in your church and well versed in your books. She had entreated him to talk with me, refute my errors, unteach me evil things, and teach me good, for he was in the habit of doing that when he found people fit to receive it. But he refused—very prudently, as I afterward came to see. He answered that I was still unteachable, being inflated with the novelty of that heresy, and that I had already perplexed various inexperienced persons with irritating questions, as she had informed him. He said, "But leave him alone for a while. Just pray to God for him. In his reading he will for himself discover what that error is and how impious it is." He disclosed to her at the same time how he himself, when a little one, had, by his misguided mother, been given over to the Manichees, and had not only read, but even written out almost all their books. He had come to see (without argument or proof from anyone) how much that sect was to be shunned, and had shunned it. When he had said that, she would not be satisfied but repeated more earnestly her entreaties, shedding copious tears, that he would see and discourse with me. He, growing a little bored and irritated, said, "Go away from me, as you live! It is not possible that the son of these tears should perish." She accepted that answer (as she often mentioned in her conversations with me) as though it were a voice from heaven.

The Death of a Friend

From *Confessions*, Book IV, 7–11

In 375, Augustine returned to his home in Thagaste to teach rhetoric, accompanied by some of his friends from Carthage. He continued as an "auditor" of the Manichees and expected his friends to follow his lead. But his life seemed suddenly meaningless when his closest fiend died.

In those years, when I first began to teach rhetoric in my native town, I had made a very dear friend from association in our studies. He was my age and, like myself, just rising up into the flower of youth. He had grown up with me from childhood, and we had been both school-fellows and play-fellows. But he was not then my friend, nor, indeed, afterward, as true friendship is. Friendship is only true in those you bind together, joined to you by *your love poured into our hearts through the Holy Spirit that has been given to us*. Still it was very sweet, being ripened by the fervor of similar studies. I had turned him aside from the true faith (which he, as a youth, had not soundly and thoroughly mastered) toward those superstitious and harmful fables that my mother mourned in me. With me this man's mind now erred, and my soul could not exist without him. But behold, you were close behind your fugitives—at once *God of vengeance* and fountain of mercies. You turn us to yourself by wondrous means. You removed that man from this life when our friendship had scarcely completed a year. It had been sweet to me above all the sweetness of my life.

Who can declare all your praise even for his own experience? What was it that you did then, O my God? *Your judgments are like the great deep!* For when, terribly sick from a fever, he lay for a long time unconscious in a deathly sweat, and all despaired of his recovery, he was baptized without his knowledge. I, meanwhile, did not mind much, presuming that his soul would not retain what was done to his unconscious body, but rather what it had imbibed from me. It happened far differently, however, for he revived and was restored. At once, as soon as I could talk to him (which I could as soon as he was able, for I never left him, and we hung too much upon each other), I attempted to joke with him. I thought he also would joke with me at that baptism he had received when mind and senses were dormant, but now knew that he had received. But he shuddered at me, as if I were his enemy. With a remarkable and unexpected freedom, he warned me that if I desired to stay his friend, I should stop speaking to him in such a way. Confounded and confused, I concealed all my emotions until he should get well and his health would be strong enough to allow me to deal with him as I wished. But he was withdrawn from my madness, that with you he might be preserved for my comfort. A few days later, during my absence, he had a return of the fever and died.

At this sorrow my heart was utterly darkened, and whatever I looked on was death. My native country was a torture to me, and my father's house a strange unhappiness. Whatever I had done with him turned into a torture without him. My eyes sought him everywhere, but they could not find him. I hated all places because he was not in them and they could not even tell me, "Behold; he is coming," as they did when he was alive and absent. I became a great puzzle to myself, and asked *my soul why* it was *cast down,* and *why* it was *disquieted within me.* But it did not know how to answer. And if I said, *"Hope in God,"* it understandably did not obey me because that dear friend it had lost was, being human, both truer and better than any fantasy it was told to hope in. Nothing but tears were sweet to me, and they replaced my friend in the dearest of my affections.

And now, O Lord, these things have passed, and time has healed my wound. May I learn from you, who are Truth, and apply the ear of my heart to your mouth, that you may tell me why weeping should be so sweet to the unhappy. Have you—although present everywhere—cast our misery far away from you? You rest in yourself, but we are disquieted with various trials. Yet unless our weeping reached your ears, we would have no hope. How do we pluck such sweet fruit from the bitterness of life, from groans, tears, sighs, and lamentations? Is it the hope that you hear us that sweetens it? This is true of prayer, for it includes a desire to approach you. But is it also in grief for a thing lost, and the sorrow that then overwhelmed me? For I had no hope of his coming to life again, nor did I seek this with my tears. I only grieved and wept, for I was miserable and had lost my joy. Or is weeping a bitter thing that gives relief only because we cannot stand the things that we enjoyed before, and only so long as we cannot stand them?

Why do I speak of these things? For this is not the time to question, but rather to confess to you. I was miserable, as is every soul held down by the friendship of perishable things—torn to pieces at their loss, and then aware of the misery that existed before ever losing them. So it was then with me. I wept most bitterly and found my rest in bitterness. Thus I was miserable, and that life of misery I counted dearer than my friend. For though I wished it could have been otherwise, I was more unwilling to lose it than him. I did not know whether I was willing to lose it even for him, as tradition says happened with Pylades and Orestes (if it was not just a made-up story). They would gladly have died one for another, or both together, it being worse than death to them not to live together. But there had sprung up in me some kind of feeling, too, contrary to this. I was wearied by life and fearful of dying. I suppose that the more I loved him, the more I hated and feared death as a most cruel enemy that had robbed me of him. I imagined it would suddenly annihilate all, as it had him. Thus, I remember, it was with me. Behold my heart, O my God! Look into me, for I remember it well, O my Hope! You cleanse me from the uncleanness of such affections, directing my eyes toward you; you *pluck my feet out of the net*. For I was astonished that other mortals lived, since he whom I loved as if he would never die was dead. I wondered still more that I, who was to him a second self, could live when he was dead. Well did one say of his friend, "You are half of my soul," for I felt that my soul and his soul were but one soul in two bodies. Consequently, my life was a horror to me because I would not live in half. And so was I afraid that if I died, he whom I had so greatly loved should die wholly.

Augustine Meets Ambrose

From *Confessions*, Book V, 23–25

In 383, Augustine moved to Rome. The next year he was appointed professor of rhetoric in Milan, where the emperor and his court actually lived. Augustine had been growing disillusioned with the Manichees but still could not accept Christian teachings as he understood them at that time. Then he began to listen to the preaching of Ambrose, the bishop of Milan.

To Milan I came, to Ambrose the bishop, known to the whole world as among the best of men, your devout servant. His eloquent speech at that time zealously dispensed to your people *the finest* of your *wheat*, the *gladness* of your *oil*, and the sober intoxication of your wine, I was unknowingly led to him by you, that I might knowingly be led by him to you. That man of God received me like a father and greeted my journeying with proper pastoral concern. I began to love him, though not at first as a teacher of the truth, which I had no hope of finding in your church, but as a man friendly to myself. I studiously listened to him preaching to the people, not with the proper motive, but trying to discover whether his eloquence came up to its reputation or flowed fuller or lower than people asserted. I hung on his words intently but was a careless and contemptuous spectator of the content. I was delighted with the pleasantness of his speech, more learned but less cheerful and soothing than that of Faustus. Of the content, however, there could be no comparison. Faustus was straying amid Manichean deceptions, while Ambrose was teaching salvation most soundly. But *"salvation is far from the wicked,"* such as I was then. Yet I was drawing nearer gradually and unconsciously.

I took no trouble to learn what he spoke, but only to hear how he spoke, for that empty care alone remained to me, since I despaired to find an accessible way to you. Yet together with the words that I prized came into my mind the things about which I was indifferent. I could not separate them. While I opened my heart to admit the eloquence of his speech, there also entered with it, bit by bit, the truths he spoke. At first, I began to see that what he said could be defended. I now understood that the Catholic faith, which I had thought defenseless against the attacks of the Manichees, might be maintained without arrogance, especially after I had heard one or two parts of the Old Testament explained allegorically. When I had taken them literally, I was killed spiritually. As I heard many places of those books expounded to me, I condemned my despair in having believed that no defense could be made to those who hated and derided the law and the prophets. Yet I did not see that I should accept the Catholic way simply because it had learned advocates who could answer objections at length and not irrationally. Nor did I see that what I did hold ought to be condemned; both sides were equally defensible. So the Catholic way did not appear to me to be either vanquished or victorious.

I earnestly bent my mind to see if in any way I could possibly prove the Manichees guilty of falsehood. If I could have conceived of a spiritual substance, all their strongholds would have been beaten down and cast utterly out of my mind. But I could not. As I more and more considered and compared things, I judged that the opinions of the majority of the philosophers concerning the body of this world and the whole of nature that the senses can perceive were more probably true. So, in the style of the so-called Academics, doubting everything and fluctuating between all, I decided that the Manichees were to be abandoned. Even in that period of doubt, I judged that I could not remain in a sect to which I preferred some of the philosophers. However, because they were without the saving name of Christ, I utterly refused to commit the cure of my fainting soul to the philosophers. I resolved, therefore, to be a catechumen in the Catholic Church, which my parents had commended to me, at least until I saw some solid ground to which I might steer my course.

When Happiness Turns Bitter

From *Confessions*, Book VI, 9–10

One of Augustine's responsibilities as a professor of rhetoric in the imperial court was to give speeches in praise of the emperor—whether the emperor deserved praise or not. Eloquence, not truth, was the test for such speeches.

I longed for honors, financial gain, marriage; and you mocked me. In these desires I underwent the bitterest hardships. You were more gracious the less you allowed anything that was not you to grow sweet to me. Behold my heart, O Lord. You want me to recall all this and confess to you. Now let my soul cling to you, which you have freed from the sticky goo of death. How wretched it was! And you irritated its wound so that, leaving all else, it might be converted to you—who are over all, and without whom all things would be nothing—converted and healed.

    How wretched I was at that time. And how you dealt with me, to make me aware of my wretchedness. One day I was preparing to recite a speech glorifying the emperor in which I would tell many a lie that would be applauded by those who knew I lied. My heart panted with these cares, and boiled over with feverish thoughts. For, while walking along one of the streets of Milan, I observed a poor beggar—with a full belly, I imagine—joking and joyous. I sighed, and spoke to the friends around me of the many sorrows resulting from our madness, since by all our exertions—including my own labor, dragging along, under the spur of desires, the burden of my own unhappiness, and by dragging increasing it—we still aimed only to gain the same level of joy that the beggar had reached before us—and we might never gain it! For what he had obtained through a few begged coins, I was scheming for by many a wretched and tortuous turning: the joy of a temporary happiness. For he did not really possess true joy, but I, with my ambitions, was seeking one much more untrue. And in truth he was joyous, I anxious; he free from care, I full of alarms. But should anyone inquire of me whether I would rather be happy or fearful, I would reply, "Happy." Again, were I asked whether I would rather be like him or like myself, I would choose to be myself, though troubled with cares and alarms. But I would answer out of stubbornness; for was it so in truth? For I ought not to prefer myself to him because I happened to be more learned than he, since I took no delight in learning, but sought rather to please others by it not to instruct, but only to please.

Away with those, then, who say to my soul, "It makes a difference where joy comes from. That beggar found his joy in drunkenness; you wanted to find it in glory." But what glory, O Lord? That which is not in you. For as his was no true joy, so was mine no true glory and it subverted my soul more. He would get over his drunkenness that same night, but many a night had I slept with mine, and risen again with it, and was to sleep again and again to rise with it, I do not know how many times. It does indeed "make a difference where joy comes from." I know it is so, and that the joy of a faithful hope is incomparably beyond such vanity. And at that time he was beyond me, for he truly was the happier man: not only because he was thoroughly steeped in high spirits while I was torn to pieces with cares, but also that he, by giving good wishes, had gotten wine while I, by lying, was following after pride. I said something like this then to my dear friends, as I often in such matters remarked on how it went with me. I found that when it went ill with me, I would fret and so double the discomfort. And if any prosperity smiled upon me, I hated to grab for it, for almost before I could grasp it, it flew away.

A Need for Self-Examination

From *Confessions,* Book VIII, 16–20

Augustine and several of his friends were living in Milan when they were visited by a fellow African named Ponticianus. Ponticianus noticed a copy of Paul's letters and began to talk about how he had been inspired by reading about the life of Antony in the desert of Egypt and of the monasteries that had grown up near him. As Ponticianus talks about the new direction his life has taken, Augustine feels forced to look at his own life.

But you, O Lord, while he was speaking, turned me toward myself, taking me from behind my back, where I had placed myself because I was unwilling to exercise self-scrutiny. You set me face-to-face with myself, so that I could see how foul I was, and how crooked and sordid, spotted and ulcerous. I beheld and loathed myself and could find no way to fly from myself. If I tried to look away from myself, Ponticianus continued his narrative, and you again placed me in front of myself, and thrust me before my own eyes, that I might *find out my iniquity and hate it.* I had known it, but acted as though I did not, winked at it, and forgot it.

But now the more ardently I loved those who had given themselves wholly to you to be cured, the more I hated myself when compared with them. Many of my years (perhaps twelve) had passed away since my nineteenth, when, on reading Cicero's *Hortensius,* I was roused to a desire for wisdom. Still I hesitated to reject simple worldly happiness and devote myself to a search that of itself I should have preferred before the treasures and kingdoms of this world (though already found) or the pleasures of the body (though close at hand)—let alone the actual finding. But I, miserable young man, supremely miserable from the outset of my youth, had asked you for chastity, saying, "Grant me chastity and self-restraint, but not yet." For I was afraid that you would hear me quickly, and deliver me too soon from the disease of desire, which I wanted satisfied rather than extinguished. I had wandered through perverse ways in a sacrilegious superstition. Not that I thought it right, but only because I preferred it to the others, which I did not seek religiously but opposed maliciously.

I had thought that I *postponed from day to day* rejecting worldly hopes and following you only because I did not see any certain direction for my course. But now I was laid bare to myself, and my conscience scolded me. "Where are you, O my tongue? Truly, you said that you were not willing to cast off the baggage of vanity for an uncertain truth. But look, now it is certain, and the burden still oppresses you. Others who have not worn themselves out with searching for it nor spent ten years and more in thinking about it have had their shoulders unburdened and gotten wings to fly away." Thus I was inwardly consumed and greatly confused with horrible shame. How I lashed my soul with scourges of rebuke to make it follow me as I struggled to go after you! Yet it drew back. It refused and would do nothing. All its arguments were exhausted and confuted. There remained a silent trembling. It feared, as it would fear death, to be held back from those usual activities that were surely killing it.

Troubled both in mind and in appearance, in the midst of this great battle that I had strongly raised up against my soul in the chamber of my heart, I grabbed Alypius and exclaimed: "What is wrong with us? What is this? What did you hear? The unlearned jump up and *take heaven by force,* and we, with much learning but no heart, see where we wallow in flesh and blood! Are we ashamed to follow because others have preceded us when instead we should be ashamed at not following?" Such words I spoke and in my excitement flung myself from him, while he gazed upon me in silent astonishment. For I did not speak in my usual tone. My brow, cheeks, eyes, color, tone of voice, all expressed my emotion more than the words. There was a little garden belonging to our lodging of which we had the use, as of the whole house. The master, our landlord, did not live there. There the storm within my breast hurried me, where no one might impede the fiery struggle I was fighting with myself. You knew its outcome, though I did not. But I was crazy to be sane, and dying to have life, knowing what an evil thing I was, but not knowing what good thing I was shortly to become. Into the garden, then, I retired, and Alypius followed me. His presence put up no barrier to my solitude. Besides, how could he desert me when I was so troubled? We sat down at as great a distance from the house as we could. I was disquieted in spirit, impatient with myself that I did not enter into your will and covenant, O my God. *All my bones* cried out to me to enter, praising it to the skies. We do not enter by ships or chariots or feet or even by going as far as I had come from the house to that place where we were sitting. For to enter there was nothing needed but to will to go, to will it resolutely and thoroughly and not to stagger and sway about this way and that with a changeable and half-wounded will, wrestling, with one part falling as another rose.

Finally, in the very fever of my irresolution, I either tore my hair, struck my forehead or, entwining my fingers, clasped my knee. I did all this because I willed it. But I did not do what I longed to do with stronger desire, and which I would have the power to do as soon as I willed it. For in such things the power was one with the will, and to will was to do, and yet was it not done. My body was more ready to obey the slightest wish of my soul in moving its limbs on command than my soul was to obey itself and gain its greatest desire by a simple movement of the will alone.

Augustine's Conversion

From *Confessions*, Book VIII, 25–30

After a brief discourse on the nature of the human will (omit-
ted here), Augustine resumes the story of his reaction to hearing
about Antony in the desert. He is still in the garden with Alypius.
(Alypius eventually became the bishop of Thagaste, Augustine's
hometown.)

So I was sick and tormented, accusing myself far more severely
than usual, tossing and turning myself in my chain until it was
completely broken. It held me still, but only slightly. You, O
Lord, drove me on inwardly by a severe mercy, redoubling the
lashes of fear and shame in case I should again back off and
that slender remaining unbroken tie should recover strength
and enchain me even tighter. For I said mentally, "Look, let
it be done now, let it be done now." As I spoke, I almost came
to a resolution. I almost did it, but I did not. I did not retreat
to my old condition but made a stand where I could catch my
breath. I tried again and was only a little short of reaching it,
and then somewhat less, and then all but touched and grasped
it. Still I did not get to it or touch it, or grasp it, hesitating to

die to death, and to live to life. The worse way, which I was used to, prevailed more with me than the better, which I had not tried. And the very moment in which I was to become another person, the nearer it approached me, the greater horror it struck into me. It did not push me back, nor turn me aside, but kept me in suspense.

My old lovers, foolishness of foolishness and *vanity of vanities,* still held me captive. They shook my fleshly garment and whispered softly, "Are you leaving us? From that moment shall we no longer be with you forever? From that moment shall not this or that be lawful for you forever?" And what did they suggest to me in the words "this or that"? What is it that they suggested, O my God? Let your mercy turn it away from the soul of your servant. What impurities did they suggest! What shame! But now I far less than half heard them. They did not openly show themselves and contradict me, but sort of muttered behind my back and furtively plucked at me as I was departing to make me look back at them. And they did delay me, so that I delayed to burst out and shake myself free from them and to jump to where I was called. A furious habit kept saying to me, "Do you think you can live without them?"

But now it said this very faintly. For on that side toward which I had set my face but trembled to go, the chaste dignity of Self-Restraint appeared to me, cheerful but not dissolutely frivolous, honestly alluring me to come and doubt nothing, while she extended holy hands full of many good examples, to receive and embrace me. There were there so many young men and women, a multitude of youth and every age, grave widows and ancient virgins. Self-Restraint herself was in all, not *barren* but the *joyous mother of children* by you, O Lord, her Husband. She smiled on me with an encouraging mockery as if to say, "Can't you do what these youths can? Do you think any of them can do it by themselves rather than by the Lord their God? The Lord their God gave me to them. Why do you stand in your own strength, and so fail to stand? Cast yourself upon God. Do not be afraid. God will not withdraw and let you fall. Cast yourself on God without fear. God will receive you, and heal you." And I blushed beyond measure, for I still heard the muttering of my old foolishness, and hung in suspense. Again she seemed to say, "Shut your ears against those unclean members of yours on the earth, so they may be mortified. They tell you of delights, but not as the law of the Lord your God does." This controversy in my heart was nothing but self against self. Alypius, sitting close by my side, waited in silence for the result of my unusual emotion.

But when, from the secret depths of my soul, a profound reflection had drawn together and heaped up all my misery in the sight of my heart, there arose a mighty storm, accompanied by as mighty a shower of tears. So that I might pour it out with all its natural expressions, I stole away from Alypius. It seemed to me that solitude was more fit for the business of weeping. So I retired to such a distance that even his presence could not

oppress me. He understood, for I believe I had spoken something, and the sound of my voice appeared choked with weeping, and in that state I had gotten up. So he remained where
we had been sitting, completely astonished. I flung myself
down, how, I do not know, under a certain fig tree, giving my
tears free flow, and the streams of my eyes gushed out, *a sacri-
fice acceptable to you*. I spoke much to you, not indeed in these
words, yet to this effect: *"You, O Lord—how long?" "How long,
O Lord? Will you be angry forever? Do not remember against us*
former *iniquities."* I felt that I was held captive by them. I sent
up these sorrowful cries, "How long, how long? Tomorrow,
and tomorrow? Why not now? Why is there not this hour an
end to my uncleanness?"

I was saying these things and weeping in the most bitter contrition of my heart, when I heard the voice of a boy
or girl—I do not know which—coming from a neighboring
house, chanting and repeating, "Take up and read; take up
and read." Immediately my expression changed, and I began
earnestly to consider whether it was usual for children in any
kind of game to sing such words. I could not remember ever
hearing anything like it. So, restraining the torrent of my tears,
I rose up, interpreting it no other way than as a command to
me from heaven to open the book and to read the first chapter
I should light upon. For I had heard of Antony, that, when
he happened to come in while the Gospel was being read, he
received the advice as if what was read were addressed to him,

"Go, sell your possessions, and give the money to the poor, and you will have treasure in heaven; then come, follow me." By this oracle he was immediately converted to you. So quickly I returned to where Alypius was sitting, for I had put down the volume of the apostles there when I rose. I grasped it, opened, and in silence read that paragraph on which my eyes first fell: *"Not in reveling and drunkenness, not in debauchery and licentiousness, not in quarreling and jealousy. Instead, put on the Lord Jesus Christ, and make no provision for the flesh, to gratify its desires."* I read no farther, nor did I need to. Instantly, as the sentence ended, as if by a light of certainty infused into my heart, all the gloom of doubt vanished away.

Closing the book, then, and putting either my finger between or some other mark, I now with a calm face told Alypius what had happened. Then he disclosed to me what had happened in him, which I did not know. He asked to look at what I had read. I showed him; and he looked even farther than I had read. I did not know what followed those verses. It was this: *"Welcome those who are weak in faith."* He applied it to himself, and showed it to me. He was strengthened by this admonition. Through a good resolution and purpose, very much in tune with his character—which was always far better than mine—without any restless delay he joined me. We went in from there to my mother. We made it known to her. She rejoiced. We told how it happened. She leaped for joy and celebrated and blessed you who are *"able to accomplish abundantly far more than all we can ask or imagine."* She saw that you had granted her more for me than she used to ask by her pitiful and most sorrowful groaning. You so converted me to yourself that I sought neither a wife nor any other of this world's hopes. I stood on that ruler of faith just as you had revealed to her in a vision many years before. You turned her grief into a gladness much more plentiful than she had desired and much dearer and purer than the gladness she used to crave through having grandchildren of my body.

A Harsh Word That Led to Grace

From *Confessions*, Book IX, 17–19

When, in telling his life story, Augustine comes to the death of his mother, Monica, he does not dwell on that moment. He writes instead about her youth, and in particular about how she was turned away from a growing drinking habit.

When we were at the Tiberine Ostia my mother died. Since I am in a hurry, I leave out a lot. Receive my confessions and thanksgiving, O my God, for innumerable things concerning which I am silent. But I will not omit anything that my soul has brought forth concerning your servant who brought me forth—in her body that I might be born to this temporal light, and in her heart that I might be born to life eternal. I will not speak of her gifts, but yours in her. She neither made herself nor educated herself. You created her, and her father and her mother did not know what kind of person was to proceed from them. It was the rod of your Christ, the discipline of your only Son, that trained her in your fear, in the house of one of your faithful ones who was a sound member of your church. Yet she did not so much attribute this good discipline to the diligence of her mother as to an aged maidservant who had carried about her father when he was an infant, the way little ones are often carried on the backs of older girls. For this reason, and on account of her extreme age and very good character, she was much respected by the heads of that Christian house. So the care of her master's daughters was committed to her, which she performed with diligence, earnestly restraining them when necessary with a holy severity and instructing them with a sober wisdom. For, except for the times when they were very properly fed at their parents' table, she would not permit them, though parched with thirst, to drink even water. Thus she took precautions against their forming a bad habit, adding the wholesome advice, "You drink water only because you cannot get at the wine. But when you are married and in charge of storeroom and cellar, you will despise water. Still, the habit of drinking will remain." By this method of instruction and power of command, she restrained the longing of their tender age and regulated the thirst of the girls to such a becoming limit that they did not long for what was not proper.

Nevertheless, a love of wine had stolen upon her—as your servant told me, her son. For when she was a responsible young woman, her parents customarily asked her to draw wine from the cask, holding the vessel under the opening. Before she poured the wine into the bottle, she would wet the tips of her lips with a little, having no taste for more than that. She did this, not from any craving for drink, but out of the overflowing

buoyancy of her time of life, which bubbles up with playful-
ness, and is, in youthful spirits, usually repressed by the gravity
of elders. And so, adding to that little a little more each day
(for *"one who despises small things will fall little by little"*) she fell
into the habit of eagerly drinking off her little cup nearly full of
wine. Where, then, was the wise old woman with her earnest
restraint? Could anything prevail against a secret disease if
your medicine, O Lord, did not watch over us? Father, mother,
and guardians may be absent, but you are present, who have
created and called us, who also work good for the salvation of
our souls through those who are set over us. So what did you
do then, O my God? How did you heal her? How did you
make her whole? Did you not evoke a hard and bitter insult
out of another woman's soul, as if taking a surgeon's knife from
your secret store, and with one thrust remove all that infec-
tion? For the maidservant who used to accompany her to the
cellar happened to fall out with her little mistress. And when
she was alone with her, she threw this vice in her face with
a very bitter insult, calling her a wino. Stung by this taunt,
she perceived her foulness and immediately condemned and
renounced it. Even as friends turn us bad by their flattery, so
enemies by their taunts often correct us. Yet you do not judge
them according to what you accomplish through them, but
according to their own purpose. For she, being angry, desired
to irritate her young mistress, not to cure her. She did it in
secret, either because the time and place of the dispute found

them alone or because she might get in trouble for letting it go on so long. But you, Lord, Governor of heavenly and earthly things, convert to your purposes the deepest torrents and guide the turbulent stream of time. You heal one soul by the unsoundness of another. So none who understand this should attribute it to their own power if another whom they wish to correct is reformed through their words.

Why Augustine Writes His Confessions

From *Confessions,* Book X, 2–4

In the tenth book of Confessions, *Augustine turns from reviewing his past to examining his present life. Here he talks about his need to confess, both to God and to others.*

O Lord, the depths of our conscience are *naked to your eyes.* What in me could be hidden from you even if I were unwilling to confess to you? I might be able to hide you from myself, but not myself from you. But now, because my groaning witnesses that I am dissatisfied with myself, you shine forth and satisfy and are loved and desired. And so I blush for myself and renounce myself, and I choose you and can neither please you nor myself, except in you. To you, then, O Lord, I am manifest, whatever I am. I have already said what it profits me to confess to you. I do it not only with words and sounds of the flesh, but with the words of the soul and the cry of reflection that your ear knows.

When I am wicked, confessing to you is nothing but being dissatisfied with myself. When I am truly devout, it is nothing but not attributing it to myself, because you, O Lord, *bless the righteous;* but first you *justify the ungodly.* My confession, therefore, O my God, in your sight, is made to you silently, yet not silently. For in noise it is silent; in affection it cries aloud. For neither do I say anything right to people that you have not already heard from me, nor do you hear anything of the kind from me that you yourself did not say first to me.

Why then should I care whether other people hear my confessions, as if they were going to *heal all my diseases?* People are curious to know the lives of others but slow to correct their own. Why do they desire to hear from me what I am, who are unwilling to hear from you what they are? And how can they tell, when they hear from me of myself, whether I speak the truth, seeing that no man knows what is in a person *except the human spirit that is within?* But if they hear anything from you concerning themselves, they will not be able to say, "The Lord lies." For if they hear from you of themselves, will they not know themselves? And how can they who know themselves say, "It is false," unless they themselves lie? But because *love believes all things,* I too, O Lord, confess to you so that others may hear. I cannot prove to them whether I confess the truth, yet they will believe if love opens their ears to me.

You, my most secret Physician, make clear to me what fruit I may reap by doing it. These confessions of my past sins— which you have *forgiven* and *covered* to make me happy in you, changing my soul through faith and your sacrament—stir up hearts when they are read and heard, so they will not sleep in despair and say, "I cannot," but rather wake in the love of your mercy and the sweetness of your grace. By grace the weak are strong, if by grace they are made conscious of their own weakness. As for the good, they delight in hearing of the past errors of those who are now freed from them. They delight, not because they are errors, but because they have been and are so no longer. For what fruit, then, O Lord my God, to whom my conscience makes daily confession, more confident in the hope of your mercy than in her own innocence—-for what fruit, I ask you, do I confess to others in your presence by this book what I am now, not what I have been? For that fruit I have both seen and spoken of, but what I am now, at the very moment of making my confessions, various people desire to know, both those who knew me and those who did not. They have heard of or from me, but their ear is not at my heart, where I am whatever I am. They want to hear me confess what I am within, where they can neither stretch eye, nor ear, nor mind. They desire it as those willing to believe. But will they understand? Love, by which they are good, tells them that I do not lie in my confessions. Love in them believes me.

The Wonders of God's Love

From *Confessions*, Book X, 38–40

Sometimes Augustine gets caught up in wonder at the amazing grace that God has shown him. This is one of those occasions.

O Fairness, so ancient, and yet so new! I loved you too late. Look, you were internal, and I external. And I looked for you in external things. Unlovely, I rushed thoughtlessly among the things of beauty you made. You were with me, but I was not with you. Those things kept me far from you, even though unless they were in you would not be at all. You called and cried aloud and forced open my deafness. You gleamed and shone and chased away my blindness. You exhaled a fragrance, and I drew in my breath and still pant after you. I tasted and still hunger and thirst. You touched me, and I burned for your peace.

When I am joined to you with all my being, then I shall have pain and effort in nothing. My life will be a real life, being completely full of you. But now, since the one you fill is the one you lift up, because I am not full of you I am a burden to myself. Joys of sorrow contend with sorrows of joy.

On which side the victory may be I do not know. Woe is me!
Be gracious to me, O Lord. My evil sorrows contend with my
good joys. On which side the victory may be I do not know.
Woe is me! Be gracious to me, O Lord. Woe is me! Look, I
do not hide my wounds. You are the Physician, I the sick one.
You are merciful, I miserable. Is not life on earth a trial? Who
wishes for difficulties? You command them to be endured, not
to be loved. For none love what they endure, though they may
love to endure. Even though they rejoice to endure, they would
rather there were nothing to endure. In adversity, I desire prosperity; in prosperity, I fear adversity. What middle place, then,
is there between these, where human life is not a trial? Woe to
the prosperity of this world, once and again, from fear of mis-
fortune and a corruption of joy! Woe to the adversities of this
world, once and again, and for the third time, from the desire
of prosperity; and because adversity itself is a hard thing, and
makes shipwreck of endurance! Is not life on earth a trial, and
that without intermission?

My whole hope is only in your exceedingly great mercy.
Give what you command and command what you will. You
impose self-restraint upon us, *"but I perceived,"* says one, *"that
I would not possess wisdom, unless God gave her to me—and it
was a mark of insight to know whose gift she was."* For by self-
restraint we, who were scattered abroad as many, are bound
up and brought into one. They love you too little who love

anything alongside you, which they do not love for you, O love, who always burn, and are never quenched! O love, my God, kindle me! You command self-restraint. Give what you command and command what you will.

The Temptation to Overeat

From *Confessions*, Book X, 43–47

Augustine is all too aware that sin is not only part of his past; he is still constantly tempted in many ways. One of the hardest is the temptation to overeat. After all, he has to eat something in order to live. The problem is knowing when to say, "Enough."

There is another *daily trouble* that I wish were *enough for today*. By eating and drinking, we repair the daily decays of the body, until you *destroy both food and stomach*. Then you shall destroy my desires with an amazing satisfaction, and shall clothe this *perishable body* with an eternal *imperishability*. But now necessity is sweet to me, and I fight against this sweetness, lest I be captured by it. I carry on a daily war by fasting, often *enslaving my body*, and my pains are expelled by pleasure. Hunger and thirst are pains of a sort. They consume and destroy like a fever unless the medicine of nourishment relieves us. Since relief is at hand through the comfort we receive from your gifts, with which land and water and air serve our infirmity, our calamity is called pleasure.

This much you have taught me: that I should bring myself to take food as medicine. But during the time that I am passing from the uneasiness of hunger to the calmness of fullness, the snare of desire lay in wait for me. The passage itself is pleasure, nor is there any other way of getting there, where necessity forces us to go. While health is the reason for eating and drinking, a dangerous delight accompanies it like a servant. This delight mostly tries to take precedence so that I may do for its sake what I say I do, or desire to do, for health's sake. And they do not have the same limit. What is sufficient for health is too little for pleasure. Often it is doubtful whether it is the necessary care of the body which still asks nourishment or whether a sensual snare of desire is waiting on us. In this uncertainty my unhappy soul rejoices and prepares an excuse as a defense, glad that it is not clear what is enough for healthy moderation. So, under the pretense of health it may conceal the business of pleasure. I try daily to resist these temptations and summon your right hand to my help. I refer my churning desire to you, because I still have no willpower in this matter.

I hear the voice of my God commanding, *"Be on guard so that your hearts are not weighed down with dissipation and drunkenness."* Drunkenness is far from me. In your mercy, do not let it come near to me. But dissipation sometimes creeps upon your servant. In your mercy, keep it far from me. No one can have self-restraint unless you give it. You give us many things we pray for, and whatever good we receive before we prayed for it, we receive from you. I was never a drunk, but I have known drunks made sober by you. So it was your doing that those who never were such might not be so, just as it was from you that those who have been so once might not remain so always. It was your gift, too, that both might know whose doing it was. I heard another voice of yours, *"Do not follow your base desires, but restrain your appetites."* And by your favor have I heard this saying likewise, which I have much delighted in, *"We are no worse off if we do not eat, and no better off if we do."* That is, neither shall the one make me abound nor the other make me wretched. I heard also another voice, *"For I have learned to be content with whatever I have. I know what it is to have little, and I know what it is to have plenty. . . . I can do all things through him who strengthens me." See* here a soldier of the celestial camp—not dust as we are. But *remember,* O Lord, *that we are dust,* and *that from the dust you have formed us. He was lost, and is found.* Nor could he do this of his own power, seeing that he whom I so loved, saying these things through your inspiration, was of that same dust. *"I can,"* says he, *"do all things through him who strengthens me."* Strengthen me, that I may be able. Give what you command and command what you will. He confesses that he has received, and when *he boasts, he boasts in the Lord.* I have heard another asking to receive: Do not let gluttony overcome me. It appears, O my holy God, that you give when what you command is done.

You have taught me, good Father, *"Everything is indeed clean, but it is wrong for you to make others fall by what you eat."* And, *"Everything created by God is good, and nothing is to be rejected, provided it is received with thanksgiving."* And, *"Food will not bring us close to God."* And no one should *"condemn us in matters of food and drink."* And, *"Those who eat must not despise those who abstain, and those who abstain must not pass judgment on those who eat."* I have learned these things, thanks and praise be to you, O my God and Master. You knock at my ears and enlighten my heart. Deliver me out of all temptation. It is not the uncleanness of meat that I fear, but the uncleanness of desire. I know that Noah was allowed to eat every kind of meat that was good for food; that Elijah was fed with meat; that John, filled with a wonderful abstinence, was not polluted by the living creatures (that is, the locusts) that he ate. I know, too, that Esau was deceived by a longing for lentils, and that David blamed himself for desiring water, and that our King was tempted not by meat but bread. The people in the wilderness deserved reproof, not because they desired meat, but because in their desire they murmured against the Lord.

Placed, then, in the midst of these temptations, I strive daily against longing for food and drink. It is not of such a nature that I am able to decide to cut it off once for all and not touch it afterward, as I was able to do with keeping mistresses. The bridle of the throat, therefore, is to be held halfway between slackness and tightness. And who, O Lord, are not in some degree carried away beyond the bounds of necessity? Whoever they are, they are great. Let them magnify your name. But I am not such a one, *"for I am a sinful man."* Yet I also magnify your name; and Christ, who has *conquered the world,* intercedes with you for my sins, counting me among the *members of the body that seem to be weaker.*

How Sin Grows in Our Hearts

From *The Lord's Sermon on the Mount*, Book I, Chapter 12

One of Augustine's earlier works is a short commentary on the Sermon on the Mount (Matthew 5–7), written in 394, the year before he became bishop of Hippo. Here he uses Jesus' words about adultery (Matthew 5:27-28) to discuss sin as consent to desire, even when not carried as far as action.

"You have heard that it was said, 'You shall not commit adultery.' But I say to you that everyone who looks at a woman with lust has already committed adultery with her in his heart." The lesser righteousness, therefore, is not to commit adultery by physical contact; but the greater righteousness of the kingdom of God is not to commit adultery in the heart. Now, one who does not commit adultery in the heart much more easily guards against committing physical adultery. So Jesus, who gave the later precept, confirmed the earlier. He came *not to abolish* the law, *but to fulfill* it. It is well worthy of consideration that he did not say, "Everyone who lusts after a woman," but, "Everyone who looks at a woman with lust," that is, who turns toward her with this aim and this intent, to feel lust; which, in fact, is not

merely to be tickled by fleshly delight, but fully to consent to lust. So the forbidden appetite is not restrained, but satisfied if opportunity should be given.

There are three things that go to complete sin: the suggestion of, the taking pleasure in, and the consenting to. Suggestion takes place either by means of memory or by means of the bodily senses—when we see, hear, smell, taste, or touch anything. And if it gives us pleasure to enjoy this, this pleasure, if illicit, must be restrained. For instance, when we are fasting and see food, the appetite of the palate is stirred up. This does not happen without pleasure. We do not consent to this desire but repress it by the right of reason, which has the supremacy. But if consent takes place, the sin will be complete and known to God in our hearts, although it may not become known to others by deed. There are, then, these steps: the suggestion is made, as it were, by a serpent, that is to say, by a fleeting, rapid, temporary movement of bodies. If there are also any such images moving about in the soul, they have been derived from outside the body. If any hidden sensation of the body besides those five senses touches the soul, that also is temporary and fleeting. So the more secretly it glides in to affect the process of thinking, the more aptly it is compared to a serpent. Hence these three stages, as I was beginning to say, resemble the transaction that is described in Genesis. The suggestion and a certain measure of persuasion are put forth, as it were, by the serpent. But taking pleasure in it lies in the carnal appetite, represented in the story by Eve. And the consent lies in the reason, represented by Adam. Once all this has taken place, we are driven forth, as it were, from paradise (that is, from the most blessed light of righteousness) into death—in all respects most righteously. For the one who puts forth persuasion does not compel. All natures are beautiful in their order, according to their gradations. But we must not descend from the higher, among which the rational mind has its place assigned, to the lower. Nor is anyone compelled to do this. Therefore, those who do it are punished by the just law of God, for they are not guilty of this without their own consent. Still, before a habit forms, either there is no pleasure, or it is so slight that there is hardly any. To yield to it is a great sin, as such pleasure is unlawful. Any who do yield commit sin in the heart. If, however, they also proceed to action, the desire seems to be satisfied and extinguished. But afterward, when the suggestion is repeated, a greater pleasure is kindled, which, however, is still much less than that which by continuous practice is converted into habit. It is very difficult to overcome this. And yet those who do not prove untrue to themselves and do not shrink back in dread from Christian warfare will get the better of habit itself under Christ's leadership and assistance.

Just as we arrive at sin by three steps—suggestion, pleasure, consent—so there are three varieties of sin itself—in heart, in deed, in habit. These are like three stages of death. The first is in the house, that is, when we consent to desire in the heart. A second is when the body is brought forth outside the gate, when assent goes forward into action. A third is when the mind is pressed down by the force of bad habit, as if buried under a mound of earth and now rotting in the grave. Whoever reads the Gospel sees that our Lord raised to life these three varieties of the dead. You may reflect what differences may be found in the very word of him who raises them. He says on one occasion, *"Little girl, get up!"* On another, *"Young man, I say to you, rise!"* On another occasion he was *greatly disturbed in spirit,* and *began to weep,* and again *was greatly disturbed,* and then afterward *"cried with a loud voice, 'Lazarus, come out!'"*

And therefore, under the category of the adultery mentioned in this section, we must understand all fleshly and sensual desire. For when Scripture so constantly speaks of idolatry as fornication, and the apostle Paul calls avarice by the name of idolatry, who doubts but that every evil desire is rightly called fornication? After all, the soul, neglecting the higher law by which it is ruled and prostituting itself for the base pleasure of the lower nature as its reward (so to speak), is corrupted. Therefore let all who themselves feel carnal pleasure rebelling against right inclination through the habit of sinning, by whose untamed violence they are dragged into captivity, recall to mind as much as they can what kind of peace they lost by sinning. Let them cry out, *"Wretched man that I am! Who will rescue me from this body of death? Thanks be to God through Jesus*

Christ!" In this way, when they cry out that they are wretched, in the act of wailing they implore the help of a comforter. It is no small approach to blessedness, when they come to know their wretchedness. Therefore, *"Blessed are those who mourn, for they will be comforted."*

How to Pray

From *The Lord's Sermon on the Mount*, Book II, Chapter 3

In this selection, Augustine discusses Jesus' words in Matthew 6:5-8 about how we should pray.

"And whenever you pray," says Jesus, *"do not be like the hypocrites; for they love to stand and pray in the synagogues and at the street corners, so that they may be seen by others."* Here also it is not being seen by others that is wrong but doing these things for the purpose of being seen by others. There is just one rule to be kept, from which we learn that what we should dread and avoid is not that others know these things, but that things be done with this intent of seeking in them the fruit of pleasing others. Our Lord himself, too, preserves the same words, when he adds similarly, *"Truly I tell you, they have received their reward."* This shows that he forbids this striving after that reward in which fools delight when they are praised by others.

"But whenever you pray," says he, *"go into your room."* What is that room but just our hearts themselves? *"Shut the door,"* says he, *"and pray to your Father who is in secret."* It is a small matter to enter into our room if the door stands open to the

unruly, so that outside things rush in and assail our inner self. We have said that outside are all temporal and visible things, which make their way through the door, that is, through our senses into our thoughts, and loudly interrupt those who are praying with a crowd of empty images. The door is to be shut and the senses to be resisted, so that spiritual prayer may be directed to the Father. This is done in the inmost heart, where prayer is offered to the Father who is in secret. *"And your Father,"* says he, *"who sees in secret will reward you,"* This had to be wound up with a closing statement like that. At this stage, the admonition is not that we should pray, but how we should pray. Jesus is giving instructions with regard to the cleansing of the heart, which nothing cleanses but the undivided and single-minded striving after eternal life from the pure love of wisdom alone.

"When you are praying," says he, *"do not heap up empty phrases as the Gentiles do; for they think that they will be heard because of their many words."* As it is characteristic of the hypocrites to exhibit themselves to be gazed at when praying, and their fruit is to please others, so it is characteristic of the Gentiles to think they are heard *because of their many words.* In reality, every kind of wordiness comes from the Gentiles, who make it their endeavor to exercise the tongue rather than to cleanse the heart. They try to transfer this kind of useless exertion even to influencing God by prayer, supposing that the Judge, just like people, is brought over by words to a certain way of thinking.

"Do not be like them," says the only true Magistrate, *"for your Father knows what you need before you ask him."* For if many words are used so that one who is ignorant may be instructed and taught, what need is there of them for God, who knows all things, to whom all things that exist speak, by the very fact of their existence, and show themselves as having been brought into existence? Even those things that are future do not remain concealed from God's knowledge and wisdom, in which both those things that are past and those things that will yet come to pass are all present and cannot pass away.

But since there are words that Jesus is about to speak, by which he would teach us to pray (however few they may be), you may ask why even these few words are necessary for God, who knows all things before they take place, *and knows what we need before we ask?* Here, in the first place, the answer is that we ought to urge our case with God, in order to obtain what we wish, not by words, but by the ideas that we cherish in our mind, and by the direction of our thought, with pure love and sincere desire. Our Lord has taught us these very ideas in words, so that by committing them to memory we may remember them when we pray.

But again, you may ask (whether we are to pray in ideas or in words) what need there is for prayer itself, if God already *knows what we need,* unless it be that the very effort involved in prayer calms and purifies our heart, and makes it roomier for receiving the divine gifts that are poured into us spiritually.

For it is not on account of the urgency of our prayers that God hears us. God is always ready to give us light, not of a material kind, but that which is intellectual and spiritual. But we are not always ready to receive, since we are inclined toward other things and are involved in darkness through our desire for temporal things. So prayer brings about a turning of the heart to God, who is ever ready to give, if we will but take what God has given. And in the very act of turning, there is effected a cleansing of the inner eye. The things of a temporal kind that were desired are excluded, so that the vision of the pure heart may be able to bear the pure light, divinely shining, without any setting or change—and not only to bear it, but also to remain in it, not merely without annoyance, but also with indescribable joy, in which a life truly and sincerely blessed is perfected.

God's Will and Our Will

From Sermon LVI, "On the Lord's Prayer"

One of Augustine's responsibilities as bishop was to instruct those who were preparing for baptism. After preaching on the Apostles' Creed, he would turn to prayer, using the Lord's Prayer as a model. This excerpt and the one following are from one of many sermons on the Lord's Prayer that have been preserved. Here, he talks about what it means for us to pray for God's kingdom to come and God's will to be done.

The words that our Lord Jesus Christ has taught us in his prayer are the rule and standard of our desires. You may not ask for anything but what is written there.

"Pray then in this way," he says: *"Our Father in heaven."* Now you see you have begun to have God for your Father. You will have him when you are newborn. Although even now before you are born, you have been conceived of his seed. You are on the eve of being brought forth in the font, the womb as it were of the church. *"Our Father in heaven."* Remember then, that you have a Father in heaven. Remember that you were born into death of your father Adam and that you are to

be born again into life of God the Father. What you say, say in your hearts. Only let there be the earnest affection of prayer, and there will be the effective answer from God, who hears prayer. *"Hallowed be your name."* Why do you ask that God's name may be hallowed? It is holy. Why then do you ask this for that which is already holy? And then when you do ask that God's name may be hallowed, do you not, as it were, pray to God for God, and not for yourself? No.

Understand it correctly, and it is for your own self you ask. For this is what you ask: that what is always in itself holy may be hallowed in you. What is "be hallowed"? Be counted holy; be not despised. So then you see that the good you wish you wish for your own self. For if you despise the name of God, it will be bad for you, and not for God.

"Your kingdom come." To whom do we speak? Will God's kingdom not come if we do not ask it? For we speak of the kingdom that will be after the end of the world. God always has a kingdom and is never without a kingdom. The whole creation serves God. But what kingdom then do you wish for? That of which it is written in the Gospel, *"Come, you that are blessed by my Father, inherit the kingdom prepared for you from the foundation of the world." Here* is the kingdom we mean when we say, *"Your kingdom come."* We pray that it may come in us. We pray that we may be found in it. For it certainly will come. But what will it profit you if it shall find you at the left hand? Therefore, here again it is for your own self that you

wish well, for yourself that you pray. This is what you long for in your prayer: that you may so live, that you may have a part in the kingdom of God, which is to be given to all saints. Therefore when you say, *"Your kingdom come,"* you pray for yourself, that you may live well. Let us have part in your kingdom. Let it come even to us, as it is to come to your saints and righteous ones.

"Your will be done." What! If you do not say this, will God not do God's will? Remember what you have repeated in the creed, "I believe in God the Father Almighty." If God is almighty, why do you pray that God's will may be done? What is this then, *"Your will be done"?* May it be done in me, that I may not resist your will. Therefore here again it is for yourself you pray and not for God. For the will of God will be done in you, though it is not done by you. In those to whom he will say, *"Come, you that are blessed by my Father, inherit the kingdom prepared for you from the foundation of the world,"* shall the will of God be done, that the saints and righteous may receive the kingdom. So also in those to whom he shall say, *"Depart from me into the eternal fire prepared for the devil and his angels,"* shall the will of God be done that the wicked may be condemned to everlasting fire. That God's will may be done by you is another thing. So it is not without cause but for your own good that you pray that God's will may be done in you. But whether it is agreeable or disagreeable to you, it will still be done in you. Oh, that it may be done by you also! Why do I say

then, *"Your will be done, on earth as it is in heaven,"* and do not say, *"Your will be done by heaven and earth"*? Because what is done by you God does in you. Never is anything done by you that God does not do in you. Sometimes, indeed, God does in you what is not done by you. But never is anything done by you if God does not do it in you.

But what is *"on earth as it is in heaven"*? The angels do your will. May we do it also. *"Your will be done, on earth as it is in heaven."* The mind is heaven; the flesh is earth. When you say (if you do say it) with the Apostle, *"With my mind I am a slave to the law of God, but with my flesh I am a slave to the law of sin,"* the will of God is done in heaven, but not yet in earth. But when the flesh is in harmony with the mind and *"death has been swallowed up in victory,"* so that no carnal desires remain for the mind to be in conflict with, when strife in the earth has passed away and the war of the heart is over and there is no more reason to say, *"What the flesh desires is opposed to the Spirit, and what the Spirit desires is opposed to the flesh; for these are opposed to each other, to prevent you from doing what you want"*—when this war, I say, is over, and all desire has been changed into love, nothing will remain in the body to oppose the spirit, nothing to be tamed, nothing to be bridled, nothing to be trodden down. The whole shall go on in peace to righteousness, and the will of God will be done on earth as it is in heaven. *"Your will be done, on earth as it is in heaven."* We wish for perfection when we pray for this.

"Your will be done, on earth as it is in heaven." In the church the spiritual are heaven; the carnal are earth. So then, *"your will be done, on earth as it is in heaven,"* that as the spiritual now serve you, so the carnal, being reformed, may also serve you. *"Your will be done, on earth as it is in heaven."* There is yet another very spiritual meaning of it. For we are admonished to pray for our enemies. The church is heaven; the enemies of the church are earth. What then is, *"your will be done, on earth as it is in heaven"!* May our enemies believe as we believe in you! May they become friends and end their enmities! They are earth; therefore are they against us. May they become heaven, and they will be with us.

Forgive Us as We Have Forgiven

From Sermon LVI, "On the Lord's Prayer"

In a later part of the sermon, Augustine talks about forgiveness—both God's forgiveness of us and our forgiveness of others.

Let us say every day in sincerity of heart—and do what we say, *"Forgive us our debts, as we also have forgiven our debtors."* It is an engagement, a covenant, an agreement that we make with God. The Lord your God says to you, "Forgive, and I will forgive. You have not forgiven; you retain your sins against yourself, not I." I pray you, my dearly beloved children, hear me, since I know what is expedient for you in the Lord's Prayer, and most of all in that sentence of it, *"Forgive us our debts, as we also have forgiven our debtors."* You are about to be baptized; forgive everything. Whatever you have in your heart against any other, forgive it from your heart. So enter in and be sure that all your sins, whether original sin into which you were born through your parents after Adam, for the sake of which you run with infants to the Savior's grace, or any later sins in your lives, by word, or deed, or thought, all are forgiven. You will go out of the water as from before the presence of your Lord, with the sure discharge of all debts.

Now by reason of those daily sins of which I have spoken, it is necessary for you to say in that daily prayer of cleansing, *"Forgive us our debts, as we also have forgiven our debtors."* What will you do? You have enemies, for who can live on this earth without them? For your own sake, love them. In no way can your enemies so hurt you by their violence as you hurt yourself if you do not love them. They may injure your estate, or flocks, or house, or your servants, or your child, or your spouse, or at most, if they are given enough power, your body. But can they injure your soul, as you can yourself? Reach forward, dearly beloved, I beg you, to this perfection. Have I given you this power? The only one who has given it is the one to whom you say, *"Your will be done, on earth as it is in heaven."* Do not let it seem impossible to you. I know, I have known by experience, that there are Christians who do love their enemies. If it seems impossible to you, you will not do it. Believe then first that it can be done, and pray that the will of God may be done in you. For what good can your neighbors' ill will do you? If they had no ill will, they would not even be your enemies. Wish them well then, that they may end their ill will, and they will be your enemies no longer. For it is not their human nature that is at enmity with you, but their sin. Are they therefore your enemies because they have souls and bodies? In this they are like you. You have a soul and so do they. You have a body and so do they. They are of the same substance as you are. Both of you were made out of the same earth and given life by the same Lord. In all this they are just like you. Acknowledge them, then, as brothers and sisters. The first pair, Adam and Eve, were our parents—the one our father, the other our mother—and therefore we are brothers and sisters. But let us leave the consideration of our first origin. God is our Father, the church our Mother, and therefore are we brothers and sisters. But you will say, my enemy is a heathen, a Jew, a heretic. I spoke about that case some time ago on the words, *"Your will be done, on earth as it is in heaven."* O church, your enemy is the heathen, the Jew, the heretic, representing the earth. If you are heaven, call on your Father in heaven and pray for your enemies. Saul was an enemy of the church. Prayer was made for him, and he became its friend. He not only stopped being its persecutor, but he labored to be its helper. And yet, to say the truth, prayer was made against him, but against his malice, not against his nature. So let your prayer be against the malice of your enemies, that it may die and they may live. For if your enemy were dead, it might seem you have lost an enemy, yet have you not found a friend. But if your enemy's malice died, you have at once lost an enemy and found a friend.

But still you are saying, "Who can do, who has ever done this?" May God bring it to effect in your hearts! I know as well as you that there are but few who do it. Those who do are great and spiritual individuals. Are all the faithful in the church who approach the altar and take the Body and Blood of Christ—are they all such? And yet they all say, *"Forgive us our debts, as we also have forgiven our debtors."* What if God should answer them, "Why do you ask me to do what I have promised, when you do not what I have commanded? What have I promised? 'To forgive your debts.' What have I commanded? 'That you also forgive your debtors.' How can you do this if you do not love your enemies?" What then must we do, brothers and sisters? Is the flock of Christ reduced to such a scanty number? If only those who love their enemies ought to say, *"Forgive us our debts, as we also have forgiven our debtors,"* I do not know what to do or what to say. Must I say to you, "If you do not love your enemies, do not pray"? I dare not say so! Pray rather that you may love them. Then must I say to you, "If you do not love your enemies, do not say in the Lord's Prayer, *'Forgive us our debts, as we also have forgiven our debtors'"!* Suppose that I were to say, "Do not use these words." If you do not, your debts are not forgiven. And if you do use them and do not act on them, they are not forgiven. In order therefore that they may be forgiven, you must both use the prayer and act on it.

Why are you forever trailing your heart along the earth? Lift up your heart; reach forward; love your enemies. If you cannot love them in their violence, love them at least when they ask pardon. Love those who say to you, "I have sinned, forgive me." If you then do not forgive them, I say not merely that you blot this prayer out of your heart, but you shall be blotted yourself out of the book of God.

Forgiving Our Enemies

From *Faith, Hope, and Love,* sections 72–77

Around 421, Augustine wrote a handbook (or "enchiridion") *of Christian faith and practice based on the Apostles' Creed and the Lord's Prayer. In this selection he is again writing on forgiveness as a form, of doing good to our enemies.*

Our Lord's saying, *"So give for alms those things that are within; and see, everything will be clean for you,"* applies to every useful act that people do in mercy. Not only, then, those who give food to the hungry, drink to the thirsty, clothing to the naked, hospitality to the stranger, shelter to the fugitive, who visit the sick and the imprisoned, ransom the captive, assist the weak, lead the blind, comfort the sorrowful, heal the sick, put the wanderer on the right path, give advice to the perplexed, and supply the wants of the needy—not those only, but those who pardon the sinner also give alms. So do those who correct with blows or restrain by any kind of discipline one over whom they have power, and who at the same time forgive from the heart the sin by which they were injured or pray that it may be forgiven, they are also givers of alms, not only in that they forgive or pray for forgiveness for the sin, but also in that they rebuke and correct the sinner. In this, too, they show mercy. Now much good is bestowed upon unwilling recipients, when their advantage and not their pleasure is consulted. They themselves frequently prove to be their own enemies, while their true friends are those whom they take for their enemies and to whom in their blindness they return evil for good. (A Christian, indeed, is not permitted to return evil even for evil.) And thus there are many kinds of alms, by the giving of which we help gain the pardon of our sins.

But none of those is greater than to forgive from the heart a sin that has been committed against us. For it is a comparatively small thing to wish well to, or even to do good to, one who has done no evil to you. It is a much higher thing, and is the result of the most exalted goodness, to love your enemy, and always to wish well to, and when you have the opportunity, to do good to, one who wishes you ill and does you harm when able. This is to obey the command of God: *"Love your enemies, do good to those who hate you, . . . and pray for those who abuse you."* But seeing that this is a frame of mind reached only by the perfect children of God, and that though all believers ought to strive after it, and by prayer to God and earnest struggling with themselves endeavor to bring their souls up to this standard, yet a degree of goodness so high can hardly belong to so great a multitude as we believe are heard when they use this petition, *"Forgive us our debts, as we also have forgiven our debtors."* In view of all this, it cannot be doubted that the implied under-taking is fulfilled if people, though they have not yet managed to love their enemies, yet, when asked by those who have sinned against them to forgive them their sins, do forgive them from their hearts. For they certainly desire to be forgiven themselves when they pray, *"as we also have forgiven our debtors,"* that is, forgive us our debts when we beg forgiveness, as we forgive our debtors when they beg forgiveness from us.

Now, those who ask forgiveness of the one against whom they have sinned, being moved by their sin to ask forgiveness, cannot be counted enemies in such a sense that it should be as difficult to love them now as it was when they were engaged in active hostility. And those who do not forgive from their hearts those who repent of their sin and ask forgiveness need not sup-pose that their own sins are forgiven by God. For the Truth cannot lie. And what reader or hearer of the Gospel can have failed to notice that the same person who said, *"I am the truth,"* taught us also this form of prayer? In order to impress this particular petition deeply upon our minds, he said, *"For if you forgive others their trespasses, your heavenly Father will also for-give you; but if you do not forgive others, neither will your Father forgive your trespasses."* If the thunder of this warning does not awaken you, you are not asleep, but dead. Yet so powerful is that voice that it can awaken even the dead.

Trifling Sins

From *Faith, Hope, and Love,* sections 79–83

In this selection, Augustine looks more deeply into the nature of sin and our tendency to count some sins as trifling or not really mattering.

There are some sins that would be considered very trifling if the Scriptures did not show that they are really very serious. For who would suppose that one who says to a brother or sister, *"You fool," will be liable to the hell of fire,* did not the Truth say so? To the wound, however, he immediately applies the cure, giving a rule for reconciliation with one's offended brother or sister: *"So when you are offering your gift at the altar, if you remember that your brother or sister has something against you, leave your gift there before the altar and go; first be reconciled to your brother or sister, and then come and offer your gift."* Again, who would suppose that it was so great a sin to observe days, and months, and times, and years, as those do who are anxious or unwilling to begin anything on certain days, or in certain months or years, because vain human doctrines lead them to think such times lucky or unlucky, if we did not have the means of estimating the greatness of the evil from the fear expressed by the apostle, who says to such people, *"I am afraid that my work for you may have been wasted"?*

Add to this that sins, however great and detestable they may be, are looked upon as trivial, or as not sins at all, when people get accustomed to them. This goes so far that such sins are not only not concealed but are boasted of and published far and wide. So, as it is written, *"The wicked boast of the desires of their heart, and those greedy for gain curse and renounce the Lord."* Iniquity of this kind is called a cry in Scripture. You have an instance in the prophet Isaiah, in the case of the evil vineyard: *"He expected justice, but saw bloodshed; righteousness, but heard a cry."* From this comes also the expression in Genesis, *"How great is the outcry against Sodom and Gomorrah,"* because in these cities crimes were not only not punished, but were committed openly, as if under the protection of the law. So it is in our own times. Many forms of sin, though not just the same as those of Sodom and Gomorrah, are now so openly and habitually practiced that not only do we dare not excommunicate a layperson, we dare not even degrade a clergyperson for the commission of them. A few years ago, I was expounding the Epistle to the Galatians. In commenting on that very place where the apostle says, *"I am afraid that my work for you may have been wasted,"* I was compelled to exclaim, "Woe to the sins of people! It is only when we are not accustomed to them that we shrink from them. Once we are accustomed to them, though the blood of the Son of God was poured out to wash them away, though they are so great that the kingdom of God is wholly shut against them, constant familiarity leads to the toleration of them all, and habitual toleration leads to the practice of many of them. Grant, O Lord, that we may not come to practice all that we cannot stop." I shall see whether the extravagance of grief did not betray me into rashness of speech.

I shall now say this, which I have often said before in other places of my works. There are two causes that lead to sin: either we do not yet know our duty, or we do not perform the duty that we know. The former is the sin of ignorance, the latter of weakness. It is our duty to struggle against these; but we shall certainly be beaten in the fight unless we are helped by God not only to see our duty, but also, when we clearly see it, to make the love of righteousness stronger in us than the love of earthly things. Eager longing for them or fear of losing them leads us, with our eyes open, into known sin. In the latter case we are not only sinners (for we are so even when we err through ignorance) but we have also broken the law. We leave undone what we know we ought to do and we do what we know we ought not to do. So we should pray not only for pardon when we have sinned, saying, *"Forgive us our debts, as we also have forgiven our debtors,"* but we should pray for guidance to be kept from sinning, saying, *"and do not bring us to the time of trial."* We pray to God, of whom the psalmist says, *"The Lord is my light and my salvation."* God my light removes my ignorance. God my salvation takes away my weakness.

Now even penance itself, when by the law of the church there is sufficient reason for its being gone through, is frequently evaded on account of weakness. Shame is the fear of losing pleasure when the good opinion of others gives more pleasure than the righteousness that leads people to humble themselves in penitence. That is why the mercy of God is necessary not only when people repent but even to lead them to repent.

Now those who, not believing that sins are remitted in the church, despise this great gift of God's mercy, and persist to the last day of their lives in obstinacy of heart, are guilty of the unpardonable sin against the Holy Spirit, in whom Christ forgives sins.

God's Justice and Mercy

From *Commentary on John's Gospel,* Treatise 33

Around 407, Augustine began to write a commentary on the Gospel of John in the form of a series of lectures or treatises. It was completed in 414. This selection is from the treatise on the story of the woman caught in the act of adultery from John 8. Jesus had told the angry mob, "Let anyone among you who is without sin be the first to throw a stone at her." The mob released the woman and dispersed.

When that woman was left alone, Jesus raised his eyes to the woman. We have heard the voice of justice; let us also hear the voice of mercy. For I suppose that woman was more terrified when she heard the Lord say, *"Let anyone among you who is without sin be the first to throw a stone at her."* But they, turning their thought to themselves and by that very withdrawal having confessed concerning themselves, had left the woman with her great sin to one who was without sin. And because she had heard this, *"Let anyone among you who is without sin be the first to throw a stone at her,"* she expected to be punished by Jesus, in whom sin could not be found. But he, who had driven back her adversaries with the tongue of justice, raised the eyes of mercy toward her and asked her, *"Has no one condemned you?"* She answered, *"No one, sir."* And he said, *"Neither do I condemn you."* Perhaps you did fear to be condemned by me, because you have not found sin in me. *"Neither do I condemn you."* What is this, O Lord? Do you therefore favor sins? Obviously not. Note what follows: *"Go your way, and from now on do not sin again."* So the Lord did also condemn something. But he condemned sins, not the person. For if he were a supporter of sin, he would say, *"Neither do I condemn you.* Go, live as you will. Be secure in my deliverance. However much you sin, I will deliver you from all punishment even of hell and from the tormentors of the infernal world." He did not say this.

Let those pay attention, then, who love this gentleness in the Lord. Let them fear God's truth. *"Good and upright is the Lord."* You love God because God is good. Fear God because God is upright. In gentleness, God said, *"I have held my peace."* But in justice, God said, *"Now I will cry out."* "The Lord *is merciful and gracious."* So God is, certainly. Add further, *"slow to anger."* Add still further, *"and abounding in steadfast love."* But fear what comes last, *"and faithfulness."* For those whom God now bears with as sinners he will judge as "in contempt." *"Do you despise the riches of his kindness and forbearance and patience? Do you not realize that God's kindness is meant to lead you to repentance? But by your hard and impenitent heart you are storing up wrath for yourself on the day of wrath, when God's righteous judgment will be revealed. For he will repay according to each one's deeds."* The Lord is gentle; the Lord is slow to anger; the Lord is gracious. But the Lord is also just. The Lord is also faithful. God gives you space for correction, but you love the delay of judgment more than the amendment of your ways. Have you been bad yesterday? Today be good. Have you gone on in your wickedness today? At any rate change tomorrow. You always have great expectations and from the mercy of God make exceedingly great promises to yourself. Has God, who has promised you pardon through repentance, promised you also a longer life? How do you know what tomorrow may bring? Rightly you say in your heart, "When I have corrected my ways, God will put all my sins away." We cannot deny that God has promised pardon to those who have amended their ways and are converted. But in the prophet where you read to me that God has promised pardon to anyone who amends, you do not read to me that God has promised you a long life.

So people are in danger from both directions: both from hoping and despairing, from contrary things, from contrary affections. Who is deceived by hoping? Whoever says, "God is good, God is merciful, let me do what I please, what I like. Let me give loose reins to my desires; let me gratify the desires of my soul." Why this? Because God is merciful, God is good, God is kind. These people are in danger by hope. And those are in danger from despair, who have fallen into grievous sins and imagine that they can no longer be pardoned even if they repent. Believing that they are without doubt doomed to damnation, they tell themselves, with the disposition of gladiators destined to the sword, "Since we are already destined to be damned, why not do what we please?" This is the reason that desperate men are dangerous. No longer having anything to fear, they are to be feared exceedingly. Despair kills these; hope, the earlier ones. The mind is tossed to and fro between hope and despair. You have to worry about letting hope kill you; that is, when you hope much from mercy, you fall into judgment. Again, you have to worry about letting despair kill you; that is, when you think that the grievous sins that you have committed cannot be forgiven you, and you do not repent. Then you incur the sentence of Wisdom, which says, *"I also will laugh at your calamity."* How then does the Lord treat those who are in danger from both these maladies? To those who are in danger from hope, God says, *"Do not delay to turn back to the Lord, and do not put it off from day to day; for suddenly the wrath of the Lord will come upon you, and at the time of punishment, you will perish."* To those who are in danger from despair, what does God say? "Whenever the wicked are converted, *none of the transgressions that they have committed shall be remembered against them."* Accordingly, for the sake of those who are in danger by despair, God has offered us a refuge of pardon. And because of those who are in danger by hope and are deluded by delays, God has made the day of death uncertain. You do not know when your last day may come. Are you ungrateful because you have today on which you may be improved? So Jesus said to the woman, *"Neither do I condemn you"*; but now that you are secure concerning the past, beware of the future. *"Neither do I condemn you"*: I have blotted out what you have done. Keep what I have commanded you, that you may find what I have promised.

Appendix

*Reading Spiritual Classics for Personal
and Group Formation*

Many Christians today are searching for more spiritual depth, for something more than simply being good church members. That quest may send them to the spiritual practices of New Age movements or of Eastern religions such as Zen Buddhism. Christians, though, have their own long spiritual tradition, a tradition rich with wisdom, variety, and depth.

The great spiritual classics testify to that depth. They do not concern themselves with mystical flights for a spiritual elite. Rather, they contain very practical advice and insights that can support and shape the spiritual growth of any Christian. We can all benefit by sitting at the feet of the masters (both male and female) of Christian spirituality.

Reading spiritual classics is different from most of the reading we do. We have learned to read to master a text and extract information from it. We tend to read quickly, to get through a text. And we summarize as we read, seeking the main point. In reading spiritual classics, though, we allow the text to master and form us. Such formative reading goes more slowly, more reflectively, allowing time for God to speak to us through the text. God's word for us may come as easily from a minor point or even an aside as from the major point.

Formative reading requires that you approach the text in humility. Read as a seeker, not as an expert. Don't demand that the text meet your expectations for what an "enlightened" author should write. Humility means accepting the author as another imperfect human, a product of his or her own time and situation. Learn to celebrate what is foundational in an author's writing without being overly disturbed by what is peculiar to the author's life and times. Trust the text as a gift from both God and the author, offered to you for your benefit—to help you grow in Christ.

To read formatively, you must also slow down. Feel free to reread a passage that seems to speak specially to you. Stop from time to time to reflect on what you have been reading. Keep a journal for these reflections. Often the act of writing can itself prompt further, deeper reflection. Keep your notebook open and your pencil in hand as you read. You might not get back to that wonderful insight later. Don't worry that you are not getting through an entire passage—or even the first paragraph! Formative reading is about depth rather than breadth, quality rather than quantity. As you read, seek God's direction for your own life. Timeless truths have their place but may not be what is most important for your own formation here and now.

As you read the passage, you might keep some of these questions running through your mind:

- How is what I'm reading true of my own life? Where does it reflect my own *experience!*
- How does this text challenge me? What new *direction* does it offer me?
- What must I change to put what I am reading into practice? How can I *incarnate* it, let this word become flesh in my life?

You might also devote special attention to sections that upset you. What is the source of the disturbance? Do you want to argue theology? Are you turned off by cultural differences? Or have you been skewered by an insight that would turn your life upside down if you took it seriously? Let your journal be a dialogue with the text.

If you find yourself moving from reading the text to chewing over its implications to praying, that's great! Spiritual reading is really the first step in an ancient way of prayer called *lectio divina* or "divine reading." Reading leads naturally into reflection on what you have read (meditation). As you reflect on what the text might mean for your life, you may well want to ask for God's help in living out any new insights or direction you have perceived (prayer). Sometimes such prayer may lead you further into silently abiding in God's presence (contemplation). And, of course, the process is only really completed when it begins to make a difference in the way we live (incarnation).

As good as it is to read spiritual classics in solitude, it is even better to join with others in a small group for mutual formation or "spiritual direction in common." This is *not* the same as a study group that talks *about* spiritual classics. A group for mutual formation would have similar goals as for an individual's reading: to allow the text to shine its light on the *experiences* of the group members, to suggest new *directions* for their lives and practical ways of *incarnating* these directions. Such a group might agree to focus on one short passage from a classic at each meeting (even if members have read more). Discussion usually goes much deeper if all the members have already read and reflected on the passage before the meeting and bring their journals.

Such groups need to watch for several potential problems. It is easy to go off on a tangent (especially if it takes the focus off the members' own experience and onto generalities). At such times a group leader might bring the group's attention back to the text: "What does our author say about that?" Or, "How do we experience that in our own lives?" When a group member shares a problem, others may be tempted to try to "fix" it. This is much less helpful than sharing similar experiences and how they were handled (for good or ill). "Sharing" someone else's problems (whether that person is in or out of the group) should be strongly discouraged.

One person could be designated as leader, to be responsible for opening and closing prayers; to be the first to share or respond to the text; and to keep notes during the discussion to highlight recurring themes, challenges, directives, or practical steps. These responsibilities could also be shared among several members of the group or rotated.

For further information about formative reading of spiritual classics, try *A Practical Guide to Spiritual Reading* by Susan Annette Muto. *Shaped by the Word: The Power of Scripture in Spiritual Formation* by M. Robert Mulholland Jr. covers formative reading of the Bible. *Good Things Happen: Experiencing Community in Small Groups* by Dick Westley is an excellent resource on forming small groups of all kinds.

CPSIA information can be obtained
at www.ICGtesting.com
Printed in the USA
FSOW04n0400210317
31959FS